PRODUCT MANAGEMENT FRAMEWORKS

What They Are and How They Impact Product Delivery

Ifra Publication

CONTENTS

ABOUT

Your team depends on you as a product manager to help them through a variety of choices and difficulties. You will learn to construct your product management philosophy in this Book, Product Management Frameworks, to build excellent products.

You'll first look at what makes good product managers different from bad ones. You'll then learn how empowered, cross-functional teams enable the finest businesses to produce enormously successful products.

Finally, you'll discover better ways to prioritise and deliver new features and products. After completing this Book, you will be equipped with the abilities and understanding of the product management frameworks required to create extraordinary products.

INTRODUCTION

Hi everyone. My name is Ifra, and welcome to my Book, Product Management Frameworks. I'm a VP of product and a product coach, and I'm excited to share with you some of the philosophies and frameworks that have powered the growth of some of the most successful companies in recent memory.

Product management is a craft whose concepts can seem simple, but take deep understanding and practice to master. This Book will teach you how to think clearly about your product with practical frameworks to maximise the impact you will have. Some of the major topics that we will cover include what separates good product managers from bad ones, how high-performance product teams are structured, how to prioritise work effectively, and how to deliver value for your customers efficiently.

By the end of this Book, you'll be able to define your own product management philosophy and you'll be equipped with frameworks that help you lead your team to build exceptional products. Before beginning the Book, you should be familiar with how products are built, particularly within the context of agile software development.

I hope you'll join me on this journey to learn how to take your product management practice to the next level with the Product Management Frameworks Book, at Amazon.

HOW GREAT PRODUCTS ARE BUILT

Welcome to Product Management Frameworks. I'm Ifra, a product leader and coach. In this Book, we're going to explore what separates exceptional product managers from the rest. We're going to get practical because your product management philosophy underpins everything, from how you make decisions and influence your stakeholders to how you ship value quickly and create delightful experiences for your customers.

The frameworks we'll discuss will cover everything from the high-level structure of your product organisation down to how you make the daily decisions that will be your responsibility as a PM. So, whether you're a product manager or interested in transitioning to product management, this Book has something for you. In the first part of this Book, we'll ask a fundamental question. As a product manager, who do you serve? And your organisation's answer will determine how effectively you can build products that are loved by both your users and customers and generate revenue for your business so it can grow in scale. Effective product managers can influence their stakeholders to achieve outcomes, even if they don't have formal line management authority.

Next, we'll look at how product organisations are structured. An organisation's product, ethos, and culture arises from how it structures its product teams. Teams tend to skew towards either top-down decision making, starting from a product vision, or bottom-up decision making, starting from insights from customers and users. The best teams combine both, using autonomous, empowered, cross-functional teams and setting clear metrics that those teams can use to measure themselves against.

In upgrading your product thinking, we'll zoom into frameworks to help you make the daily prioritisation decisions that characterise the role of the product manager. There are many different tools to choose from, and the key is not to treat them as formulas, but as ways to structure your decision making and make tradeoffs when considering different types of work. We'll look at frameworks to assess your place in the market, dissect your users journey through your product, and deal with the uncertainty inherent in comparing different ideas.

In delivering value faster, we'll discuss different approaches to product delivery. Part of a product manager's role is to help their team deliver value to customers quickly, and that involves a delicate balancing act of giving the team what they need now and planning for the future. Throughout the Book, we'll follow Globomantics, a fictional company developing project management software, looking at how they might apply the philosophies and frameworks we discuss. Finally, we'll put all that we've learned together and look at how Amazon developed a set of product management philosophies and frameworks that has delivered exceptional results.

At the end of the Book, you'll have everything you need to define your own product management philosophy and the frameworks you need to excel in your role. You can also use the companion workbook to this Book to help you apply the concepts to your own context. We've got an exciting journey ahead of us, so let's get started.

WHO DO YOU SERVE?

There are many different perspectives on the role of the product manager in an organisation and in their specific product team. When thinking about your own product management philosophy, it's important to acknowledge that adopting a philosophy that is contrary to your organisation's perception of the role is going to make your life difficult. With that in mind, let's look at some of the different ways organisations view the product manager's role.

Traditionally, the project manager's role has been to serve the business. In this mode, the product manager functions like a specialised project manager, taking directions from the organisation's leadership and translating their high-level directives into work that is sufficiently defined to enable the rest of the product team to work on it. In larger, traditional organisations that have adopted agile principles, the product owner role can often look like this. The day-to-day for this type of product manager involves grooming the product backlog. Backlog grooming is an important task that we'll look at in more detail later in this Book.

Ensuring that work has been correctly prioritised and that work at the top of the backlog has been clearly scoped and defined is crucial to enabling a team to work efficiently. However, there is a flaw in this model, and it's a big one. The leadership of an organisation may not be best placed to decide where the biggest improvements to the product can be made. For one thing, executives are busy people and have all sorts of demands on their attention. They may have been close to customers at one point, but they will likely spend a fraction of their time talking with them now, and what time they do spend is with strategically important accounts. And finally, the time they do spend with those customers is likely talking about a range of things, only a few of which may directly pertain to the product.

The result is that the executives typically have a skewed or incomplete view of what the product needs. Perhaps an important client has complained to them recently about some aspect of the product or a new account was lost due to a missing feature or the organisation missed its revenue targets for the quarter. Those most recent conversations tend to find their way to the top of the backlog until another piece of feedback or critical issue comes in and takes the top spot. The outcome of this is the product team being forced to change time continually. In this model, the product manager is a messenger with no real influence on the quality of the message. What is the alternative to this traditional model of product management?

One is to reframe the product manager's role as a servant of the customer. In this model, the product manager is mandated to deeply understand the customer's needs and the problems that we can solve for that customer. There are a bunch of techniques that a project manager can use to develop this understanding. They can interview current and prospective clients to understand their context, business challenges, and goals. They can work with functions that directly interface with the customer, such as sales and customer success, to understand how the product is being perceived now. And they can use the data collected about product usage to understand where customers are finding value in the product.

Over time, the product manager should become an expert in

the customer and their needs. More than that, they should be able to identify the common threads between customers, the problems that are consistently felt, and, therefore, if solved appropriately by the product, can be a market opportunity. This customer-centric model of product management solves some of the issues we discussed with the business-centric model. First, the product manager can develop a deeper and more sophisticated understanding of the customer, which should then enable them to define better solutions to customer problems than the executives. Second, the product manager can collate data points in a systematic way, lowering the chances of big swings in prioritisation.

In short, the product manager can truly act as a voice of the customer and make sure the product is being developed to maximise customer value. If a product is adding significant value to the customer, then it should be successful. In my opinion, the customer-centric model of product management is more effective than the business-centric model. But the highest performing companies don't stop there. There is a third model of product management, and we'll discuss that model in the next chapter.

THE CEO OF THE PRODUCT

The best companies acknowledge that it's not enough for products to make money or to delight customers. Successful products have to delight customers in ways that also generate business value. For that reason, product managers have to be experts in the customer and also the different facets of the business. This product management philosophy can be summed up in Ben Horowitz's description of the product manager as the CEO of the product.

Now, this is a somewhat controversial framing, so let's spend a little bit of time unpacking it. CEOs are the ultimate responsible party for the success or failure of a company. As a result, they must understand all facets of the business and take ownership of driving the success of the company. Product managers should similarly take responsibility for driving the success of their product and take responsibility if it fails. The true breadth of this responsibility is summed up well by Marty Cagan's product risks: the risk that the product simply does not deliver value to the customer or end user, the risk that the end user cannot figure out how to use the product, the risk that it is not technically feasible to build the product, the risk that the product is not viable for the business, for example due to legal, compliance or financial constraints, and finally, the risk that the product as designed is not ethical.

Considering all these factors resolves a number of tensions inherent in the serve the business and the serve the customer product management philosophies. By defining the product manager's success simply in terms of the success of the product, the product manager must take a long-term, outcome-focused perspective. Simply responding to customer requests is not enough because sometimes customers do not know what they want. Pursuing incremental improvements to the product will result in failure if the company needs dramatic improvements to meet its goals. Adding features without considering the larger hole can lead to product bloat. Even if each feature added value by itself, if the overall product suffers, then that's on the product manager.

It's important to acknowledge that the CEO of the product philosophy places a very high standard on the product manager. Product managers operating in this mould must be polymaths and exceptionally high performers. So, if you are looking to work for an organisation that adopts this view of product management, there's a few things to keep in mind. The first is that nobody can be excellent at everything. Just as CEOs have backgrounds and strengths in a particular business discipline, so will product managers. They may have a business background, a design background, an engineering background, and so on. Understanding which disciplines are most valued by your organisation is helpful for setting yourself up for success.

Particular products may require a PM who is highly technical or who really understands behavioural science or is comfortable with bringing an early concept to life. The second is that there is a fundamental difference between the product manager as CEO and the real CEO, and that is authority. As a product manager, your team typically does not report to you; therefore, to get things done, you cannot dictate terms. You must influence your colleagues and inspire them to rally behind the vision and strategy that you are pursuing. Finally, the need to influence without authority means that building trust is crucial. You cannot be an effective product manager without the trust of your team and your stakeholders in the business. You must be able to speak each of their languages and show them that you understand their goals, needs, and perspectives. In the rest of this Book, we'll dive into the practical frameworks that can help you succeed as the CEO of the product model.

The truth is, many companies do not operate this way, so we'll follow a fictional company, Globomantics, as they attempt to transition from their old way of doing things to this new model. To begin, we'll look at how the best teams are structured to create highly successful products.

BUILDING AN EFFECTIVE PRODUCT ORGANISATION

L et's turn to how high performing product teams are organised for success. In the last chapter, we discussed three product management philosophies, the serve the business philosophy, the serve the customer philosophy, and the serve the customer in ways that work for the business philosophy.

Now we'll explore how these philosophies manifest in how product organisations are structured. All organisations have a vast array of choices when it comes to their products. Most organisations have many different types of customers that they can serve. Each of those customer groups have all sorts of problems that they are looking to solve, and there are many ways to solve each of those problems. How do organisations identify which customers, problems, and solutions to pursue?

The first way is by setting a vision and strategy. An organisation that is passionate about reducing the cost of healthcare probably shouldn't be building a product for teenagers to share videos with their friends. Setting a vision and strategy focuses the organisation and its teams on some things to the exclusion of others. For a minute, think about your own product organisation.

Can you articulate the product vision? Can you describe the different elements of the product strategy? How often do you reference your vision and strategy when making decisions day to day? It can be tempting to think of setting a vision and strategy as a purely top-down process and, therefore, serve the business exercise.

Indeed, if you are a product leader, defining an inspiring product vision and a clear strategy is hugely important and will be a major influence on how your product managers act on your behalf. Your vision must be grounded in some fundamental insight about what your customers want. Likewise, your strategy must be informed by insights, otherwise it's simply a guess masquerading as something more. Vision and strategy require both a serve the business and a serve the customer mindset. If you are a product manager, search for an organisation whose vision you find compelling and inspiring and the strategy that flows logically from that vision and what you know about the market the company operates in. If the vision and strategy is sound, you're likely to find a product management philosophy that is sound too. If not, then look elsewhere. In the CEO of the product philosophy, the product team is empowered to solve customers' problems in the ways that they think are best because they are closest to the customer.

As a result, companies that adopt this model will typically set metrics for each team that flow from the product strategy. These metrics serve as a north star for the team to measure their success against, enabling them to determine if their solutions are working. I explore this topic in more detail in two of my other Books, Exploring Positioning Product Metrics, and its sequel, Positioning Product Metrics. As we continue through this chapter, I'll highlight a few other areas where we go into greater detail in those two Books. Some organisations use this sequence of strategy to metrics to individual solutions or tactics as their primary framework for making product decisions. If that sounds interesting to you, then consider the impact mapping technique.

Impact mapping is a collaborative, strategic planning technique that takes a high-level goal, the actors that can influence or are influenced by the goal, and the impact or behaviour changes that we are hoping to facilitate for those actors. Work can then be defined in the context of this map of goals to actors to impacts to make sure it will help move the product in the right direction. Framing deliverables in this way makes it relatively easy to define metrics to assess the success of a new product or feature based on the desired impact. Further information on impact mapping can be found in the workbook that accompanies this Book, and we'll cover alternative techniques in the next chapter.

ORGANIZING
PRODUCT TEAMS

A s the organisation grows, multiple product teams will form, and this provides another opportunity to define the philosophy of the organisation through team focus and resource allocation. Let's take Globomantics as an example and assume it has two product teams. One might focus on the core product and another on growth, or it might have one focused on the existing product and market and another on finding an entirely new market.

It might split them by mobile app and web or user experience and platform or freemium and paid. Each of these choices makes implicit decisions about what aspects of the product Globomantics considers important, and the size and composition of these teams takes this even further. For example, if Globomantics had 80% of its product, design, and engineering resources working on its core product and 20% working on growth initiatives, that would suggest that its focus is largely on building new functionality rather than maximising the functionality that already exists. As a product organisation grows, so does its complexity.

Expanding from a single founding team to multiple teams can introduce inter-team dependencies. If the lines between these teams are not clearly defined, it takes work to define a structure that gives team members autonomy and a clear purpose that doesn't conflict with the autonomy of other teams. And, Of course, these are not decisions that can be made solely by the product organisation. The technology and design teams will also have a say in where their resources are allocated. It is crucial that product, design, and engineering are all aligned about where resources are to be spent. This is why a clear and agreed upon strategy is so important.

ORGANISING AROUND INSIGHTS

An organisation's product philosophy also manifests in its bottom-up processes, particularly regarding how it interacts with customers and generates and acts on insights. Every product organisation has its own norms around how decisions are made and what influences those decisions. For organisations with a command and control structure, the primary factor in a decision is the seniority of the people involved in the decision.

The opinion of the most senior person is the one that will win. As we discussed previously, driving decisions by seniority is a poor fit for product decisions because this means the decision makers are often those furthest from the customers and users we are trying to build the product for. Instead, some organisations practise the customer is always right principle. In this model, decisions are made by soliciting feature suggestions from users and customers, aggregating those suggestions, for example by allowing people to upvote suggestions, and then implementing the top ideas. This approach has a number of pitfalls too.

First, taken together, the most requested features may not add up to a coherent product. Features need to work together as a whole or else the product will feel confusing, complex, and cluttered. Second, the loudest voices may not correspond to your target market. Perhaps those who are asking for new features are customers that will never really be satisfied by our product, or otherwise don't fit your business model. And third, there may be a better way to solve the problems and frustrations that users are trying to solve through their suggestions. This approach is really a way of abdicating responsibility for making tough product decisions by passively accepting users' suggestions.

The irony is, this is just as bad for those users as it is for your business. Instead, we need to look at ways to gather insights about what users really want and need and then design solutions that meet those needs. We'll look at two ways to do this, using design thinking and using quantitative data.

DESIGN THINKING

To design great solutions for your users, you need to understand them. Product teams develop this understanding through discovery. Steve Blank describes this as getting out of the building because the only way to develop this understanding is by talking and interacting with real users. There are many frameworks for discovery work, including the lean startup methods which Steve Blank was instrumental in defining.

For today, we are going to focus on design thinking, specifically the version practised by Stanford's d.school. The design thinking process follows five phases, which are empathise, define, ideate, prototype, and test. The empathise phase is all about building empathy with your users. This can mean talking with users, observing them or immersing yourself in their environment to gain insights into their perspective. This stage is crucial for building the awareness that your views and assumptions are not the same as your users. The define phase structures the insights you've gained from the empathise phase. You can synthesise your findings into documents like user personas and empathy maps. These form a body of knowledge that you and your team can refer back to as a reminder to walk in the shoes of your user.

In addition to structuring insights around your target user, you also want to outline what insights you have generated about the problems your users want solved. Examples here include the jobs to be done framework, which frames products in terms of the job that the user is hiring the product to do. For example, both Adobe Photoshop and Instagram aim to make photos taken by users look great. But the job that most people hire Photoshop for is to edit their photos to make them look professional, whereas people hire Instagram to make it easy to share their photos with their friends and followers. Your ultimate goal for this phase is to craft a human-centred problem statement, a problem in your users' words that you are going to attempt to solve.

The ideate phase is all about challenging your assumptions and creating ideas for innovative solutions to the problem statement. One way to start is to take everything you've learned from the previous phases and start writing out how we might make statements. How might we frame ideas as questions, thereby leaving the team open to multiple possible answers or solutions to the question. Another useful technique is crazy eights where you sketch eight ideas in as many minutes on a sheet of paper. This rapid fire sketching forces you to move beyond the initial idea or ideas you have in your head to consider other alternatives. Once you have come up with some ideas, you need to converge on a single, cohesive idea that effectively solves your users' problem. An effective way to do this is to develop a number of prototypes. Prototypes can be developed cheaply and quickly so you can iterate based on the insights you gather.

The final phase, testing, gets your prototype in front of users so you can see how they interact with it. I cover the specifics of how to set up this sort of test in the final chapter of my Book, Exploring Positioning Product Metrics. There are a number Of courses on Amazon that go into much greater detail on each of these phases of the design thinking process. For our purposes, it's important to note how following a process like design thinking encourages you and your product team to develop new product ideas in a deliberative, thoughtful, and human-centred manner. As a result, your solutions will be better able to solve your users needs.

DERIVING INSIGHTS
FROM DATA

As your product matures, the data generated by the product itself, usage data, experimentation, and in-application user feedback, can provide an ongoing feedback loop between you and your users. Let's take Globomantics as an example. Globomantics sells project management software, and projects can be managed in all sorts of ways. Capturing the actions a user takes when they are using the product can help Globomantics identify features that are used heavily or not.

It can also help identify where users are confused, for example navigating back and forth between two menu options before taking an action. Over time, it's even possible to identify key actions that are predictive of longer term success with your product, such as heavier product usage, upgrading to a paid tier, and so on. If you can identify these actions, then they can be converted into metrics that can serve as a team's North Star as we discussed earlier. Tracking user actions also forms the basis for experimentation within your product. By testing new functionality against a control group, you can start to move away from hunches about what works to evidence about what works.

If you're in an organisation that tends to emphasise the most senior person's decision, then experiment data can be a good antidote as long as you can define, launch, and analyse the experiment quickly enough. I discuss experimentation in more detail in the final chapter of Positioning Product Metrics. In-app feedback tools can help you gather insights from users and customers at a specific point in their journey, for example after their first time encountering a new feature or after they have been using the product for a certain period of time. This in the moment feedback is not the same as being able to sit with the user and observe them interacting with the product, but it is less invasive, time consuming, and can be deployed at scale.

Product analytics is a growing field, and there are more and more tools available to help you set up the necessary infrastructure. Some of the more established players are Segment, Amplitude, Heap, and Pendo. It's important to note that product analytics will rarely give you a true sense of why certain user behaviour is occurring, even though it can give you a granular picture of what is happening. To get to the why, there is still no substitute for getting out of the building and talking with users.

THE EMPOWERED PRODUCT TEAM

A ll the data gathered from these bottom-up processes, from qualitative insights such as those surfaced through design thinking through to quantitative insights gathered from product analytics, serve as a rich source of insight to drive a product strategy and the daily direction of a product team. It is one more reason why empowering the team to make decisions rather than prescribing a direction to them is effective.

The best product organisations artfully blend the top-down processes and bottom-up processes that we have discussed in this chapter. By setting a clear vision and strategy, product leadership can make sure all product teams are moving in the same direction in the service of the wider company objectives. By remaining open to the team's insights gathered from product discovery, the product organisation can adapt as market, user or product needs change. In other words, these two processes inform each other. Strategy informs where to focus discovery, and the insights we gather should in turn inform the strategy. The same principles we discussed for the product manager role in the previous chapter apply to the product team as a whole.

Organisations are most successful when they set up a framework that balances direction with flexibility based on insights and measures the success of the team based on the outcomes it achieves rather than its output or efficiency. Empowering the team to explore and then make decisions is the secret source of high-performing product teams. Now that we've covered the philosophical and organisational underpinnings of high-performing product organisations, let's dive into the day-to-day. In the next chapter, we'll look at a variety of frameworks to help you make better prioritisation decisions so you can focus your team's efforts on the initiatives that will drive the biggest impact.

UPGRADING YOUR PRODUCT THINKING

L et's now look at some common frameworks for one of the most important tasks a product manager faces, prioritisation. Note that when I talk about prioritisation, I'm not talking about ordering items on your team's backlog. As a product manager, you are faced with all sorts of constraints, time, money, capabilities, and ultimately you need to decide how to spend your resources most wisely.

To make matters even more difficult, you never have perfect information with which to make decisions. So, while you'll need to decide whether to build feature A or feature B, you'll also need to decide whether to explore idea C or idea D or to invest more time in customer discovery or ideation. Balancing the different factors that play into your product investment decisions is hard. Do you spend time fixing bugs or building the next great thing? Do you cater to the whims of a big enterprise client or dozens of smaller clients that each bring in a fraction of the enterprise client's revenue? Do you bet big on moonshots or play things safe through optimizations? Do you spend time building for scale or move as fast as possible?

In this chapter, we'll explore a number of different frameworks. They all have a different perspective on how to think about your product and what is most important. Unlike the previous chapters where I presented some philosophies as less effective than others, you can think of these frameworks as tools that you can use to sharpen your decision making in different contexts. Let's dive in.

OPPORTUNITY-SOLUTION TREES

First up, let's look at the opportunity solution tree. Developed by Teresa Torres, it is a way to visualise potential avenues you could take, from your desired outcome through opportunities, possible solutions, and finally, experiments to test those solutions. It helps you to map out the possibilities and make sure you are considering multiple options.

Let's walk through an example with Globomantics as our case study. First, we need to decide what our desired outcome is. For Globomantics, this may be to increase engagement in their project management tool. Next, we need to outline the opportunities we see to increase engagement. These opportunities should be coming from your user research, so let's frame them as such. Some opportunities might be I want to keep track of my daily tasks across all my projects or I want to collaborate with my team on the different tasks for my project or simply I want somewhere to store all of my documents related to my project in a logical way.

Some opportunities might be bigger or broader than others, and often they can be grouped. So you may have a mini-hierarchy of opportunities. When doing this activity yourself, map your opportunities out in categories that make sense for your team. It may take you a couple of iterations to get this right. Even these first few steps of the tree are helpful because you can now prioritise the higher order opportunities. Which opportunity is the most valuable to pursue? Once you've made that decision, we can go deeper into the more granular opportunities. Maybe Globomantics decides it wants to pursue the opportunity of helping its users organise their tasks.

Underneath this, we can consider tackling the opportunities associated with managing tasks across projects, within projects, across team members, and so on. Eventually, we will get down to a subset of opportunities that are specific enough to develop solutions for. Here's where the next branch of the tree occurs. We want to avoid considering just a single idea per opportunity. For example, there's many ways we might enable a project manager to better manage tasks that are assigned across the team. We might give them a view of all the tasks due today or this week or by team members so they can identify who will need help, or we may give them metrics so that they can assess each team member's historical performance completing tasks. Or, we may enable them to tag team members on tasks to notify them of a question so they can unblock at-risk tasks more quickly.

All of these are potential solutions to the same opportunity, even though they are quite different. How do we decide which solution to pursue? We can use experiments. Experiments are about testing assumptions, and each of the solutions Globomantics is considering are built on assumptions. By testing the largest assumptions out for each solution, we can get a sense of which one is the most likely to deliver the most value to our project managers. Opportunity solution trees are powerful because they allow you and your team to visualise and structure your thinking. Rather than just throwing ideas around and letting opinions win the day, you can use this structure to identify your overall objective and work down from there, prioritising as you go and making sure you don't just jump in on the first idea that is thrown out.

STORY MAPPING

Next, let's talk about story mapping. This concept was developed by Jeff Patton and rethinks the concept of a backlog. When you think of a backlog, you probably think of a list of items like user stories and epics in something like Jira. Like I said earlier, as product people, we need to prioritise. We always have more things we'd like to build than we have time for.

In a backlog, the most important stuff goes at the top. Simple. Well, Jeff says that's a broken system, and here's why. When you simply organise all your stories by priority, you lose the context for those stories. How do they fit into the larger picture of your product? If you evaluate each story in isolation, there's a good chance that your product will end up being a bag of bits. Story mapping is an attempt to solve this problem. Rather than placing user stories in a linear backlog, it places them along the user's journey through your product. Like we did with the opportunity solution tree, let's walk through how a story map works.

We'll start with the high-level activities that a user does in your product. Place them in order of when they occur in your users' journey. If you already have a user journey map, that's a good place to start. For Globomantics, our high-level activities might be setting up a new project, inviting the rest of the team to collaborate, defining the tasks in a project, and tracking the project progress towards going live. If you're unsure which orders some user activities happen in, take a look at your user data or make an educated guess. The important thing is to get these high-level activities down on paper. Because these activities are macro things that a user does in a product, they're often the essentials of your product. There's no prioritisation at this level because each of these activities are required to some degree.

Without one of these activities, there's no functioning product. Next, start plotting the smaller tasks on your story map under the activities. These are the more specific things that a user does to complete the larger activity. Just as epics break down into stories in a typical backlog, a similar concept applies here. For example, under the invite the team activity, users might want to invite coworkers via an email with onboarding steps. They might want to be able to define access levels for newly invited users, be able to see that someone has successfully created an account, and so on. You can also start to prioritise at this stage, placing the most essential tasks closer to the top. In theory, taking a thin slice of the most essential stories gives you a coherent minimum viable product.

The next layer could be a version 2, and so on. Viewing the whole user journey when making these decisions helps ensure that you are focusing on the user experience as a system and not as a series of isolated features. The opportunity solution tree and the story map share a common theme. They are about visualising the work that you and your team are doing and prompting discussion about what is really important with users and outcomes at the centre of that discussion. One of the great things about story mapping is that you're probably already familiar with its component parts, the user story. So try it out. It's a way of upgrading your thinking and team conversations without much extra work.

RICE

Next, let's talk about RICE. The RICE framework was developed by Intercom and stands for reach, impact, confidence, and effort. Unlike the opportunity solution trees and story mapping, the output of RICE can be a linear list of prioritised features. You can calculate a RICE score by multiplying reach, impact, and confidence together and dividing by effort.

I personally prefer to use RICE as more of a thinking tool to make sure you're looking at different ideas through some basic criteria. Let's take a look at each element of RICE. First is reach, which is an assessment of the number of customers or users this idea will affect in a given time period. Some ideas may seem really cool, but only for a small set of users. Others may seem more banal, but have a much broader appeal or relevance. RICE gives you a method for considering this in your analysis. In most cases reach should be quantifiable based on your existing product data. For example, in a given month, you could look at how many people access the part of the product where this idea is located, or you could look at how many people reach the relevant step in the funnel, and so on.

The I in RICE is for impact, which is the degree to which the idea is likely to improve your customers' experience and move you in the direction of your goal. Impact may be harder to measure than reach, but you can typically compare ideas on the impact dimension. Some ideas might be micro optimizations, whereas others might be transformational changes. We'd like to assume a different degree of impact in these cases. Confidence allows you to weigh your reach and impact estimates by how much evidence you have for them. Ideas come from all sorts of places, some developed from rigorous research while others come from teammates, stakeholders, users, and so on. That also means that some are more fleshed out and some have better backing than others.

Using confidence in your ranking allows you to deprioritize the hot new idea that has little evidence behind it, or you could choose to prioritise a small research project to gather more data on that particular idea. In either case, considering confidence helps you to make that assessment rather than being blinded by novelty. Finally, effort. Effort is a measure of your team's resources. How many person days is an idea estimated to take? Obviously the Holy Grail is an idea that has high reach, impact, and confidence and low effort. Most ideas fall at different points on all those dimensions. Effort is the counterweight to the other factors that reflect the fact that you have limited resources. Let's evaluate a few Globomantics features with RICE.

Both of these features relate to Globomantics' consulting customers. These customers have projects with multiple different clients, so they need ways to make sure clients can only see their own projects. One possibility is to give these customers the ability to set access explicitly for each user and project. Another is specific to other Globomantics customers and allows the customer and their client to each work on their collective project in their own Globomantics account. We could probably estimate the reach of these features based on what Globomantics knows about its customers. Thirty percent of its customers may be consultants with multiple projects in their account, for example. The cross-org collaboration feature might have lower reach because it requires both parties to already be using Globomantics.

We might estimate the impact of both of these features as high because there are no good workarounds for these customs right now. Having to create separate accounts or work in someone else's Globomantics account are both high friction activities that pull the user out of their usual workflow. As a result, we may be pretty confident in our estimates. Finally, we can look at effort and see that the access policies feature is much simpler to implement. Taken together, it looks like that feature is much more attractive from our RICE analysis. However, don't use RICE blindly. There may be good reasons to still pick a feature that scores a bit lower on this assessment.

For example, if 10% of customers that are targeted by the cross-org collaboration feature are large, high value customers, then Globomantics might want to focus its efforts on delighting them even if other features might have a wider reach on paper. Up next, we'll look at how your customers' perceptions of features can help you prioritise and how those perceptions can change over time as the market evolves.

THE KANO MODEL

The Kano model was developed by Professor Noriaki Kano in the 1980s. It helps us assess how satisfied customers might be with different features we are considering. Kano's model considers features on two axes, satisfaction and functionality. Satisfaction is obviously our goal for our customers, and this axis ranges from delight to dissatisfaction or frustration.

The functionality axis measures how much of a feature the customer gets and how well we've implemented it. To achieve full functionality will require significant investment, so this axis can also be thought of as the degree of investment we make in the feature. With these two axes, we can explore Professor Kano's insights into the different kinds of possible features we could build. Firstly, we have the simplest relationship between satisfaction and functionality, performance features. With these features, customers are more satisfied the more they get out of the feature. For Globomantics, an example might be the amount of storage space each account is given.

The more storage Globomantics gives customers, the more satisfied they will be. Second, we have threshold features. These can also be called must-have features because they are features that customers expect. If our product doesn't have these features, then it will be considered bad or incomplete by customers. Conversely, if we fully implemented these features, we won't have satisfied customers per se, we'll have just avoided them being dissatisfied. The good news is that even a little investment in these features goes a long way to increasing satisfaction, even though we'll never cross that midline with these features alone. For Globomantics, a threshold feature might be the ability to create projects and tasks within them.

It simply wouldn't be a project management tool without that basic functionality. Third, and potentially most interesting, are delighter features. These features are almost like the inverse of our threshold features. The absence of threshold features is keenly felt by customers in a negative sense. By contrast, customers don't really notice the absence of delighter features because they are unexpected. But these features have the potential to be your secret source because they can create huge increases in customer satisfaction with even a little investment. All wildly successful products have introduced the world to some new, delightful feature. Think about the iPhone's touch screen, for example. Identifying these delighter features is hard, and you can't simply look at others and copy them.

Globomantics will need to work hard to develop new ways to delight its customers in the crowded project management software market. The market for your product isn't static, however. When someone releases a truly delightful feature, others will copy it and it will start to become another threshold feature. The touchscreen pioneered by Apple is now ubiquitous, for example. As a cloud-based Software as a Service company, Globomantics is following the playbook that Salesforce developed for CRM software. Salesforce's no software model was delightful when it was introduced and has led to Salesforce's explosive growth. But think about what might happen if Globomantics decided that that model was too difficult and it instead wanted to return to the days of selling its software on CDs. I don't think customers would consider it for a moment.

For Globomantics, a cloud-based model is a threshold feature. So, how can you use the Kano model? It is not a tool to prioritise all types of product work because it is intentionally focused on customer satisfaction. Professor Kano's model will not tell you if you should pay down some technical debt or conduct a full-scale redesign of your existing product, for example. But the model can help you identify what features you will absolutely need in your product, which may be a source of competitive advantage and which may actually be a bad idea because customers are indifferent to them, or worse.

A common implementation of the Kano model proposed by Kano himself is to turn it into a questionnaire. By surveying your target users, you can start to plot your feature hypotheses on the Kano model rather than relying on guesswork. An example question set is included in the Book workbook.

PRIORITISATION FRAMEWORKS - SUMMARY

L et's review the different prioritisation frameworks we just covered and look at some common themes. The first thing to note is that the four models we discussed are just a few of the many frameworks out there that can help you make product investment decisions. Each has their own perspective on what the most important factors in product decision making are because no one framework can consider everything.

To even try would be to create a very inflexible and bloated prioritisation process. For example, opportunity solution trees are a discovery tool. They are designed to help you navigate from an outcome and consider a wide range of possibilities in a structured way. By contrast, RICE is a lightweight extension of the typical value versus effort calculation. It is designed to help you consider basic tradeoffs between features. The second thing to note is that using one of these frameworks allows you to approach prioritisation questions systematically rather than from opinion or gut feel. This is important as they also give you a method for communicating the reasons behind your eventual decision. If someone disagrees with a decision, they can reference the logic inherent in the model you've used or propose an alternative framework that might approach the decision in a different light.

Finally, I want to highlight some common ground across the frameworks, namely that they emphasise the customer or user of the product, they place value on data as inputs into the analysis, and they prompt conversation. For example, story mapping encourages prioritisation based on the user's journey through the product while RICE encourages us to think about the customer's reach and impact. When it comes to data, Kano's model is easily translated into a practical questionnaire, and opportunity solution trees emphasise running experiments to test potential solutions, and each of them encourages discussion with your team, whether it's a round of visualisation or in discussing the inputs to how the ideas have been prioritised.

I encourage you to try out these different models and see how they change and inform the conversations you have with your product team. By involving your team using these frameworks, you'll help them refine their own thinking about your product and help empower each team member to better contribute. Personally, I use them all at different times and for different purposes to help my teams think through particular prioritisation decisions they face based on our strategy and the maturity of the product in question. Next, we'll turn to product delivery and how your team can deliver value fast.

DELIVERING VALUE, FASTER

N ow let's turn to where a lot of teams start: product delivery. We aren't going to spend a ton of time here for two reasons. First, there are already a number Of courses on Amazon that go into the frameworks we're going to discuss in a lot more detail. Second, product delivery flows from the product discovery and prioritisation frameworks that we have just discussed. Getting the how of product delivery right is irrelevant if you can't clearly articulate what you need to build and why.

The purpose of a product delivery framework is to ensure that our product team ships high-quality product releases. A great idea with flawed implementation is just as useless as a bad idea executed flawlessly. Recently, it's become fashionable for organisations to proclaim that they follow the agile methodology.

An entire industry of certification, coaching, and transformation consultants has developed to serve this shift. It's also become fashionable to proclaim that organisations are getting agile wrong, misinterpreting it, or not staying true to its spirit. So, as we have done in other chapters of this Book, let's go back to first principles and look at why different product delivery frameworks exist and what their strengths and weaknesses are.

WATERFALL

The first delivery framework we'll consider is waterfall. In the early days of software development, new product initiatives were treated as projects. This makes sense in a service business model where the key consideration is delivering a set of requirements on time and on budget. The waterfall framework is so called because it progresses through a series of linear stages, requirements gathering, design, development, testing, and deployment.

In this model, changes to scope are problematic because they disrupt the plan. Documentation and careful upfront planning are therefore essential in this model. If you have ever worked with a third-party software development company, then this general sequence will probably sound familiar. This is because delivering against tightly defined scope which outlines exactly what must be built is more predictable and easier to quote for than the messy business of committing to achieving a particular outcome such as an improvement in a product KPI. Many internal product teams are the same way, this is because project-based thinking is easy to understand and feels right.

It makes sense to plan the work before you start it. It makes sense to test something you've built. It makes sense to try and avoid deviating from your plan and losing focus, and your plan may seem like the obvious way to achieve the outcome you are looking for. But there is a practical reality that has resulted in so many companies undertaking the journey of agile transformation. Firstly, projects never progress exactly according to plan. Software is complex, and you learn things as you go that would have been hard to identify in planning.

Second, the linear process encourages a handoff mindset, that means the experts in later phases, such as designers and engineers, can't provide critical input on earlier phases. And finally, bringing new products to life is an inherently uncertain endeavour. The linear process means that until the whole product is built, we have nothing of value for customers.

AGILE

L et's contrast the Waterfall method of product development with Agile. Agile emphasises working software as the measure of progress released frequently. This means finding ways to break up work into smaller batches that deliver incremental value. Agile also emphasises that the definition of value comes from the customer. The software must satisfy them. Breaking work into small batches has a number of advantages over the Waterfall framework.

First, releasing software early and often allows teams to get feedback from customers much earlier and iterate based on that feedback. There is no better way to assess value than putting products in users' hands. Second, working in smaller increments actually improves estimations of work. Humans are notoriously bad at estimating how long something will take. So it's common in Agile to use story pointing. Story points provide a relative assessment of effort compared to some reference work that has previously been completed. Tracking story points over multiple iterations allows teams to determine their velocity and therefore make better estimates in future iterations.

Third, working in small batches reduces the need for reams of documentation because the team can identify what needs to be done through regular collaborative conversation. There is no need for complex timelines and requirements documents because the goal is always to ship the next useful iteration of the software and then respond to feedback. Consequently, Agile also emphasises the importance of self-organising teams, as these teams can respond quickly to the feedback they receive on their regular releases.

In this way, Agile naturally brings teams closer to an empowered product team model. However, Agile is not a silver bullet. For one, there are times when making a truly big bet may be called for, and attempting to pursue this big bet by shipping small increments may not make sense. We'll explore this a bit more in our Amazon case study later on. Agile also assumes a knowledge of the customer and their problems, but does not provide a framework for product discovery despite its importance. If a team uses Agile processes, but has limited customer interactions and only demos its working software internally until a big release, then it is likely to share many of the shortcomings of Waterfall. Next, let's look at Dual-track Agile, which addresses some of these concerns.

DUAL-TRACK AGILE

Dual-track agile extends the typical Agile methodology to include discovery alongside delivery. In other words, it attempts to provide a process to answer the question of what we should build in a way that stays true to Agile's principles. Dual-track agile is so called because there are two parallel tracks in this model, discovery and delivery. The delivery track is the part that is typical Agile, estimating work that's already been decided upon, prioritising it, and then delivering it.

The discovery track is the new component and is concerned with validating ideas, in other words, identifying what ideas should be passed over to the delivery track. As we discussed when we talked about the RICE prioritisation framework, you will often have varying levels of confidence in different product ideas, and validating ideas is an iterative process. Just as Agile is a response to the reality that detailed plans rarely pan out as written, dual-track agile reflects the reality that discovery work is non-linear and inherently unpredictable, too. If you knew in advance that an idea will be successfully validated after a certain time period, then what is the need for those validation activities? So what does dual-track agile look like in practice?

Let's take a look at how a typical sprint might look for Globomantics, our makers of project management software. Based on the opportunity solution tree, the team might be focused on the task management aspects of the product. On the discovery side, the product manager, tech lead, and product designer might be conducting interviews with project managers, both existing users and prospective users, to understand in more detail how they think about task management. They might also be conducting a usability test of an early prototype for a team's task due today's screen that shows a project manager or the task coming due and who is responsible for them.

Meanwhile, the rest of the team may be building out the functionality that has some degree of validation. They might be constructing a test to see if the ability to tag users and tasks improves task completion. Or maybe that test has already been run, and now they are proceeding to full implementation of the feature, including all the necessary logging, analytics, error handling, performance optimization, and so on. It's important to note that the two tracks of dual-track agile should inform each other. It's not just discovery that impacts delivery. We should be building features in such a way that we can continue to learn once they are delivered. For example, maybe users responded well to the mentions feature in our testing, but once the feature was launched, only a small subset of users mentioned another user in the first week. That might mean users are not aware of the functionality, so we need to do a better job of highlighting it, or that we inadvertently interviewed only power users when testing the idea, and other users are not interested in using it. Regardless, we can feed these insights back into the discovery track to continue to iterate.

No framework is perfect, but hopefully you can see that dual-track agile does a good job of combining the rapid insight generation and idea validation afforded by discovery techniques with the efficiency and adaptiveness of Agile delivery. The result is dramatically less wasted time and effort for your team and the ability to deliver meaningful results faster. We're almost at the end of this Book. To conclude, we'll tie everything we've discussed together in a case study looking at how Amazon has created a product organisation that has resulted in transformational growth and market-leading products in multiple industries.

LEARNING FROM
THE BEST

L et's pool together everything we've learned through the lens of one highly successful company, Amazon. As is hopefully clear by now, there is no one right product management philosophy or framework, although there are some common principles that high-performing product teams adhere to. Amazon's product philosophy is very different to Google's, which, in turn, is very different to Apple's. So this case study is just one way of doing things, not the way. One caveat before we dive in.

I have not personally worked for Amazon. However, a lot has recently been written about Amazon's product culture, particularly in Working Backwards by Bill Carr and Colin Bryar, which is a great read if you're interested in diving deep into Amazon's culture and ways of working. Let's start with Amazon's overall product philosophy. Amazon is well known for being customer obsessed, going to great lengths to improve its customers' experience. Examples of this just in the area of shipping include Amazon's relentless drive to get customers' goods to them faster with 2-day and, more recently, 1-day shipping and providing customers credits for digital goods when they voluntarily choose slower shipping.

Capturing and then passing on those cost savings rather than simply pocketing them as profit is true customer obsession. At the same time, another Amazon principle is to deliver results. As we'll see, Amazon is very metrics driven, and it has been able to achieve its scale through a relentless drive to be more efficient in its core operations. In other words, its culture marries customer centricity with business acumen. And let's think about scale for a second. Amazon's rise has been truly meteoric. Its leaders are encouraged to think big and have a bias for action, and this is displayed in the speed of the company's growth. Its leaders are owners that insist on high standards and work to earn trust from their teams and stakeholders. And they have implemented a strict set of hiring standards known as the Bar Raiser to ensure that every Amazon product manager is exceptional.

All of these traits are common to the CEO of the product model we discussed at the start of this Book. Now let's look at how product teams are structured at Amazon. Amazon builds single-threaded teams, which means the team is focused on one thing and one thing only. As Ifra Limp, Amazon's SVP of devices, said, "The best way to fail at inventing something is by making it somebody's part-time job." Having teams with a single focus, led by a leader with the necessary skills and experience enables teams to work autonomously. Amazon takes the concept of autonomous, empowered teams even further, giving these leaders the remit to decide on the composition of their team as well, how many people are needed, with what skills, and so on. As Carr and Bryar describe in Working Backwards, metrics are developed for each team to give them a north star to measure the success of their work.

Specifically, these metrics are input metrics which can be controlled by the team. Input metrics are similar to leading indicators, because they should drive output metrics like revenue or NPS, and unlike output metrics, teams can truly own them and be accountable for them. Amazon has a highly data-driven culture as a result, and teams are encouraged to constantly run experiments to identify ways to improve their input metric.

Amazon works hard to define the right input metric for each team, iterating on them until they find a definition that encourages the right mindset from the team.

In this example, the early metric encouraged teams to produce as many product detail pages as possible with the thinking that more choice is good for customers. But those pages are useless if they aren't used or if the product is not in stock. Subsequent definitions encouraged the team to focus on the end goal of providing customers with choices that they could actually purchase.

AMAZON CASE STUDY, PART TWO: FRAMEWORKS

A mazon has popularised a number of distinct frameworks to help it make decisions. These frameworks help Amazon make high-quality decisions despite the challenges posed by its vast scale and rapid growth. Amazon strongly favours the written word for decision making because it removes the bias of how effective someone is at presenting from the evaluation of an idea or decision. Amazon's two primary written frameworks are the six page memo and the PR/FAQ. The six page narrative adds constraints to the evaluation of a decision. Six pages forces concepts to be flushed out to a certain level of detail without going overboard.

Amazon's perspective is that a six page narrative document allows for greater discussion of the nuances of an idea than a typical presentation would. Six page narratives are refined extensively through feedback, and therefore, serve as both documentation for an idea and a method for evaluating the idea's quality. Over time, Amazon has identified useful principles within the six page narrative itself. For example, Amazonians will often include tenets in their six page narratives, which can be used to clearly outline underlying principles and state key decisions that have been made previously. This allows discussion about a narrative to start from a common ground. If people do not agree on the tenets, then what follows is irrelevant until those differences are resolved.

The press release and FAQ or PR/FAQ for short is a key framework for Amazon's product organisation and the document behind the title of car and Briar's book working backwards. The idea is that when product teams come up with an idea for a new product, they start by writing a press release for that product and work backwards from there to get to the details of what needs to be built. The PR/FAQ stems from Amazon's principle of customer obsession. By framing the idea as a press release, it forces teams to think first about how to delight customers. In light of the press release, the value being delivered by a new product must be clear and succinct. The FAQ component puts the idea through the ringer further by asking the tough questions that customers and internal stakeholders will want to know the answers to.

External questions might include how much the product will cost and how it works. Internal questions might include why this is a problem that needs to be solved right now, what dependencies there are, and what the unit economics of the product are expected to be.

Amazon Case Study, Part Three: Comparing Amazon to "Best Practice"

Let's compare Amazon's approach to the usual descriptions of product management best practice. At first glance, Amazon's approach may feel similar to Waterfall with its heavy reliance on upfront documentation. Indeed, the six-page narrative and PR/FAQ documents are a far cry from the user stories typically used by teams practising Agile, but it's important to note the intent of these documents and the process surrounding them.

The intent of the PR/FAQ, for example, is to clearly articulate the value a product idea is supposed to deliver for a customer and to lay bare the underlying assumptions. That is very different from a product requirements document that assumes a product idea is valuable and focuses instead on the specifics of what needs to be built. The end result of a Waterfall process is that the thing will be built, regardless of whether it delivers value or not. In contrast, the end result of the PR/FAQ document is often that the idea is not built, because the case for building the product is not compelling enough. PR/FAQs will be refined repeatedly by teams and even then, most will never proceed to implementation. In this way, PR/FAQs are used as a prioritisation tool to make sure Amazon only works on ideas that have a high likelihood of delivering customer value.

In terms of product delivery, Amazon has at times spent years developing new products before releasing them to market. This ethos is a very far cry from the small-batch ethos of Agile and has been credited with runaway successes such as Amazon Web Services, as well as failures such as the Fire Phone. Amazon's principles are hard to master and can sometimes be intention, and like any company, Amazon can veer from its own principles. In the case of the Fire Phone, Amazon's principle of customer obsession, coupled with its focus on refining ideas through its internal processes, meant it assumed it knew what its customers wanted. As a result, they did not leave the building and built a product that emphasised features that customers did not care about. But all told, Amazon's principles of team empowerment, exceptionally high leadership standards, customer centricity, and metrics-driven decision making has served it well.

The company has been wildly successful at bringing multiple new products to market and defining entirely new product categories such as cloud computing with AWS, e-readers with Kindle, and voice-activated assistants like Alexa. It has done this by defining its own coherent and high-performing product philosophy supported by a series of powerful product frameworks. The point of this case study is not to suggest you carbon copy Amazon's approach. Instead, my hope is that it serves as inspiration for you to define your own product-management philosophy and frameworks to help you and your team create awesome products that improve the lives of the people you are looking to serve.

CONCLUSION

L et's provide a brief recap of what we covered in this Book. We divided our thinking into two parts, with each having two subsections. In the first part, we discussed product management philosophies around the product manager role and the product organisation. Organisations typically see the role of the product manager as there to serve the business, serve the customer, or serve the customer in ways that work for the business.

This typically influences how much autonomy and responsibility the product manager is given for the success or failure of their product. High-performing product organisations are typically composed of autonomous, empowered, cross-functional teams. They are guided by a mix of top-down and bottom-up thinking, starting with a clearly articulated vision and strategy and being informed by qualitative and quantitative insights from customers and users. In the second part, we discussed frameworks for validating and prioritising product ideas and taking those ideas from concepts to fully implemented products and features. There is no one right way to evaluate and prioritise product ideas, and each framework has its own set of underlying assumptions.

Consider using a framework that emphasises discovery, such as opportunity solution trees, story mapping, or impact mapping, and consider using frameworks that structure your comparison of different ideas to help you make clear-eyed decisions, such as RICE or Kano analysis. You don't need to stick religiously to one framework, and, like Amazon, you can develop your own. Finally, we looked at how to deliver value to your customers and users quickly. We compared waterfall, agile, and dual-track agile. Here again, the most important factor is to develop a process that works best for your team and emphasises the product philosophy you want to foster.

With any process, people can follow the letter of the law without adhering to its underlying principles, so start from your product philosophy and work with your team to bring that philosophy to life. I hope this Book has been valuable for you and prompted you to think deeply about how you and your team practice product management in your own organisation. If you want to go deeper, I encourage you to check out the companion workbook to this Book. And as always, if you have any questions or feedback, please reach out to me. Thank you for reading.

www.ingramcontent.com/pod-product-compliance
Lightning Source LLC
Chambersburg PA
CBHW071110220526
45467CB00004B/1772